PIANO · VOCAL · GUITAR

JENNIFER KNAPP
THE COLLECTION

ISBN 0-634-08060-1

HAL·LEONARD®
CORPORATION
7777 W. BLUEMOUND RD. P.O. BOX 13819 MILWAUKEE, WI 53213

Visit Hal Leonard Online at
www.halleonard.com
www.gotee.com

A LITTLE MORE

Words and Music by
JENNIFER KNAPP

Moderately

Turn Your eyes ___ from on this way. ___
For all the sin that lives in me,

I have proved ___ to live a das-tard-ly day. I ___
it took a nail to set ___ me free. Still, ___

hid my face ___ from the saints ___ and the an-
what I do ___ I ___ don't ___ wan-na do ___

UNDO ME

Words and Music by
JENNIFER KNAPP

Moderately

Pa - pa, ___ I think I messed up a - gain. ___ Was it some - thin' I did or was it some -

- thin' I ___ said? ___ I don't mean ___ to do ___ you wrong; it's just the way ___

___ of hu - man na - ture. Sis - ter, ___ I know I

BREATHE ON ME

Words and Music by
JENNIFER KNAPP

Guitar: Drop D tuning:
(low to high) D-A-D-G-B-E

SAY WON'T YOU SAY

Words and Music by
JENNIFER KNAPP

INTO YOU

Words and Music by
JENNIFER KNAPP

Driving Rock

She's a skin art junk-ie, ___ all
cute and pe-tite. ___ All her fat - cat schemes, don't look a-round, _ don't you
e-ven blame _ me. It's a real bad thing to spill _ your shades _ for a

THE WAY I AM

Words and Music by
JENNIFER KNAPP

Blind these eyes __ who nev - er tried __ to lose __ temp - ta - tion.

I'm so scared; __ oh, where's __ the hes - i - ta - tion? __

You so eas - i - ly proved that You could save a man; __ well, I am __

LAY IT DOWN

Words and Music by
JENNIFER KNAPP

Moderately fast

Seeing as I found a rock in my
Pride can break a man right down from i-

pock-et,   seeing as I found
ron,   twist him 'round, 'round and

a glitch in my soul.
tat-ter up a soul.

This the ho-ur of _____ my heal - ing, of _____ my heal - ing, yeah. _

Yeah, _____ oh.

My heart, _____ my heart _____ re - deemed. _

Lay it down, lay it down _____ yeah. _____

WHOLE AGAIN

Words and Music by
JENNIFER KNAPP

HOLD ME NOW

Words and Music by
JENNIFER KNAPP

*Recorded a half step lower.

MARTYRS & THIEVES

Words and Music by
JENNIFER KNAPP

Lyrics:

There's a place in the dark-ness that I _____ used to cling _____ to; it press-es harsh _____ hope a-gainst _____ time.

ghosts from my past _____ who've owned _____ more of my soul _____ than I thought I had _____ giv-en a-way.

nev-er been much _____ for the bear-ing of soul _____ in the pres-ence of _____ an-y man. _____

DIAMOND IN THE ROUGH

Words and Music by SHAWN COLVIN
and JOHN LEVENTHAL

REFINE ME

Words and Music by
KIM BONTRAGER

WHEN NOTHING SATISFIES

Words and Music by
JENNIFER KNAPP

BY AND BY

Words and Music by
JENNIFER KNAPP

*Recorded a half step lower.

ROMANS

Words and Music by
JENNIFER KNAPP

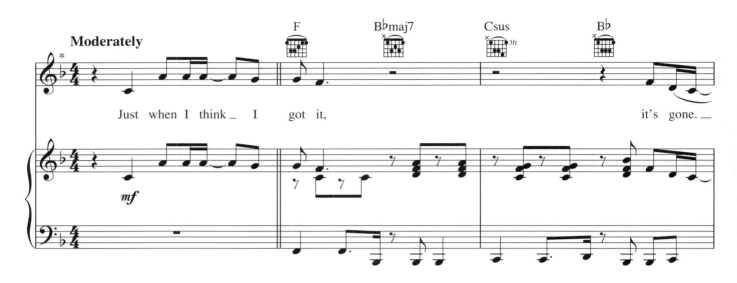

Just when I think __ I got it, it's gone. __

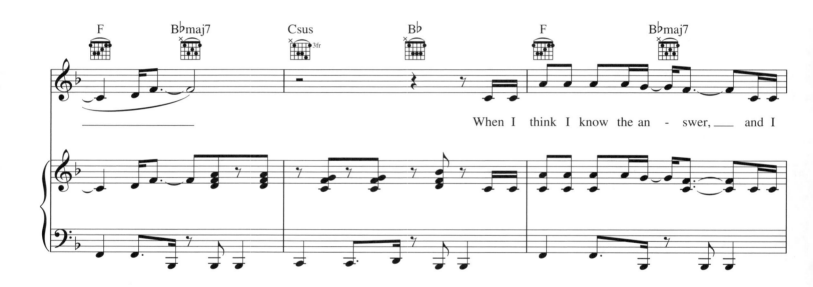

_____ When I think I know the an - swer, ___ and I

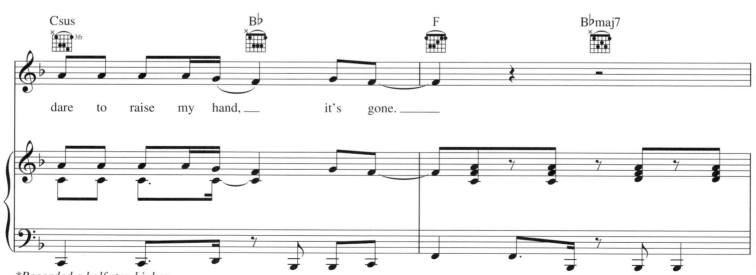

dare to raise my hand, ___ it's gone. _____

*Recorded a half step higher.

No, I don't have to ___ be ___ con - demned; ___ Je - sus saved me from ___

Solo ends

___ the laws ___ of sin. ___ If I fall, I'll try ___ a - gain. ___

___ With the Spir - it as my guide, _ yeah, with the Spir - it as my guide, _ I will not ___

Instrumental solo

More Contemporary Christian Folios from Hal Leonard

AVALON – THE CREED

Our matching folio to the very latest from this popular CCM vocal quartet features photos and all ten songs: Abundantly • All • Be with You • The Creed • Far Away from Here • The Good Way • I Bring It to You • Overjoyed • Renew Me • You Were There.

_____ 00306601 Piano/Vocal/Guitar $14.95

WAIT FOR ME – THE BEST FROM REBECCA ST. JAMES

Our matching folio to the first best-of compilation from Aussie gospel artist Rebecca St. James includes 16 previously recorded songs: Breathe • God • Here I Am • I Thank You • Lamb of God • Mirror • Pray • Psalm 139 • Reborn • Song of Love • Speak to Me • Stand • Wait for Me • and more.

_____ 00306546 Piano/Vocal/Guitar $14.95

JEREMY CAMP – STAY

The *All Music Guide* says CCM newcomer Jeremy Camp "delivers one of the most awe-inspiring performances of any debut CCM artist in the past decade" and calls *Stay* "vocally, musically and lyrically ... a potent mix of one standout cut after another." Our matching folio features all 12 tracks: All the Time • Breaking My Fall • In Your Presence • Nothing • Right Here • Stay • Take My Life • Understand • Walk by Faith • and more.

_____ 00306565 Piano/Vocal/Guitar $14.95

KEITH GREEN – THE ULTIMATE COLLECTION

Our 20-song collection matches Sparrow's latest compilation CD of the late, great Keith Green, who died in a plane crash in 1982. Includes: Asleep in the Light • I Can't Believe It • I Want to Be More like Jesus • Jesus Commands Us to Go • Make My Life a Prayer to You • My Eyes Are Dry • Oh Lord, You're Beautiful • Pledge My Head to Heaven • Rushing Wind • Soften Your Heart • There Is a Redeemer • You Are the One• You! • Your Love Broke Through • and more.

_____ 00306518 Piano/Vocal/Guitar $16.95

JENNIFER KNAPP – THE WAY I AM

Includes all 12 tunes from the critically acclaimed CD: Around Me • Breathe on Me • By and By • Charity • Come to Me • Fall Down • In Two (The Lament) • Light of the World • No Regrets • Say Won't You Say • Sing Mary Sing • The Way I Am.

00306467 Piano/Vocal/Guitar $14.95

TWILA PARIS – HOUSE OF WORSHIP

Includes 12 songs : Christ in Us • Come Emmanuel • Fill My Heart • For Eternity • Glory and Honor • God of All • I Want the World to Know • Make Us One • Not My Own • We Bow Down • We Will Glorify • You Are God..

_____ 00306517 Piano/Vocal/Guitar $14.95

JEFF DEYO – LIGHT

All 13 songs from the second solo release by the former Sonicflood frontman: As I Lift You Up • Bless the Lord • I Am Yours Forever • I Fear You • I Love You • Keep My Heart • Ray of Light • Sacrifice of Praise • Show the Wonder • Take Me to You • These Hands • We Come to Your Throne • Your Name Is Holy.

_____ 00306603 Piano/Vocal/Guitar $14.95

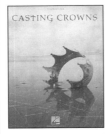

CASTING CROWNS

Matching folio to the Steven Curtis Chapman-produced eponymous debut from this adult contemporary Gospel group. Features 10 songs: American Dream • Glory • Here I Go Again • If We Are the Body • Life of Praise • Praise You with the Dance • Voice of Truth • What If His People Prayed • Who Am I • Your Love Is Extravagant.

_____ 00306621 Piano/Vocal/Guitar $14.95

BETHANY DILLON

All 11 songs from the self-titled Sparrow CD from this critically acclaimed 15-year-old singer/songwriter: Aimless • All I Need • Beautiful • Exodus • For My Love • Great Big Mystery • Lead Me On • Move Forward • Revolutionaries • A Voice Calling Out • Why.

_____ 00306636 Piano/Vocal/Guitar $14.95

PHILLIPS, CRAIG AND DEAN – LET YOUR GLORY FALL

Our matching folio features all ten inspirational tunes from this popular CCM trio's 2003 release: Every Day • Fall Down • Hallelujah (Your Love Is Amazing) • Here I Am to Worship • How Deep the Father's Love for Us • Lord, Let Your Glory Fall • My Praise • Only You • What Kind of Love Is This • The Wonderful Cross.

_____ 00306519 Piano/Vocal/Guitar $14.95

NICHOLE NORDEMAN – WOVEN & SPUN

Includes all 11 songs from the 2002 release of this Dove Award nominee: Doxology • Even Then • Gratitude • Healed • Holy • I Am • Legacy • Mercies New • My Offering • Never Loved You More • Take Me As I Am.

_____ 00306494 Piano/Vocal/Guitar $14.95

Prices, contents and availability subject to change without notice.

ZOEGIRL – DIFFERENT KIND OF FREE

Our matching folio features all 11 songs: Beautiful Name • Contagious • Different Kind of Free • Feel Alright • Inside Out • Life to Me • Love Me for Me • She • Unbroken • Wait • You Get Me.

00306562 Piano/Vocal/Guitar $14.95

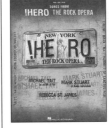

SONGS FROM !HERO THE ROCK OPERA

Selections from the popular touring musical that asks the question, "What if Jesus had been born in Bethlehem ... Pennsylvania?" This folio presents 15 selections from this modern-day version of the greatest story ever told. Songs, by today's most popular CCM artists, include: Fire of Love • Hero • I Am • Kill the Hero • Lose My Life with You • Manna from Heaven • Raised in Harlem • Secrets of the Heart • and more.

_____ 00306634 Piano/Vocal/Guitar $14.95

THIRD DAY: WIRE

13 songs: Billy Brown • Blind • Come On Back to Me • I Believe • I Got a Feeling • I Will Hold My Head High • Innocent • It's a Shame • Rock Star • San Angelo • 'Til the Day I Die • Wire • You Are Mine.

_____ 00306629 Piano/Vocal/Guitar $14.95

DC TALK – INTERMISSION: THE GREATEST HITS

17 of DC Talk's best: Between You and Me • Chance • Colored People • Consume Me • Hardway (Remix) • I Wish We'd All Been Ready • In the Light • Jesus Freak • Jesus Is Just Alright • Luv Is a Verb • Mind's Eye • My Will • Say the Words (Now) • Socially Acceptable • SugarCoat It • Supernatural • What If I Stumble.

_____ 00306414 Piano/Vocal/Guitar $14.95

STEVEN CURTIS CHAPMAN – DECLARATION

13 songs: Bring It On • Carry You to Jesus • Declaration of Dependence • God Follower • God Is God • Jesus Is Life • Live Out Loud • Magnificent Obsession • No Greater Love • Savior • See the Glory • This Day • When Love Takes You In.

_____ 00306453 Piano/Vocal/Guitar $14.95

SWITCHFOOT – THE BEAUTIFUL LETDOWN

All 11 songs from the CD by these San Diego-based Christian alt-rockers: Adding to the Noise • Ammunition • Beautiful Letdown • Dare You to Move • Gone • Meant to Live • More Than Fine • On Fire • Redemption Side • This Is Your Life • Twenty-Four.

_____ 00306547 Piano/Vocal/Guitar $14.95

0804